# See for Your Self

*by*

## Douglas Florian

Richard C. Owen Publishers, Inc.
Katonah, New York

# Meet The Author

Richard C. Owen Publishers, Inc.
PO Box 585
Katonah, New York 10536

Library of Congress Cataloging-in-Publication Data

Florian, Douglas.
   See for your self / Douglas Florian.
      p. cm. – (Meet the author)
   ISBN-13: 978-1-57274-821-7
   ISBN-10: 1-57274-821-4
      1. Florian, Douglas—Juvenile literature. 2. Authors, American—20th
century—Biography—Juvenile literature. 3. Children's literature-Authorship-Juvenile
literature.  I. Title: See for your self. II. Title. III. Meet the author (Katonah, N.Y.)

   PS3556.L589Z473 2005
   811'.54-dc22
   [B]
2005048830

ISBN 978-1-57274-821-7

ISBN      1-57274-821-4


Color separations by Leo P. Callahan, Inc., Binghamton, New York

Printed in the United States of America

9       8       7       6       5       4       3       2       1


For more information about our collection of Meet the Author books
visit our website at www.RCOwen.com or call 800-336-5588.

*To my parents*

I grew up on an island: the island of Manhattan.
Manhattan is a part of New York City, one of the busiest,
noisiest, and most crowded cities in America,
but I love it.

I love the museums, and the parks, and the people,
and the food, and sometimes, I even love the noise.
I'm lucky to live and work in New York City,
where every day is different.

I'm also lucky because I grew up in a happy family,
a family surrounded by art.

My father was, and still is, an artist. When I was a kid
I used to watch him create great works of art. He would
draw and paint people and places, parks, and streets.
Sometimes he would even draw me. And sometimes
I would draw him.

I also liked to take photographs with my dad's camera.
Here, I'm photographing my brother and two
of our friends. The building in the background
is where I live today, although I have lived
in many other places.

When I was 10 years old I entered a national
coloring contest.  Out of thousands of entries,
I was awarded Third Prize—a pair of gold-plated
roller skates.  I rode those skates until all the gold paint
had peeled off, and then some.

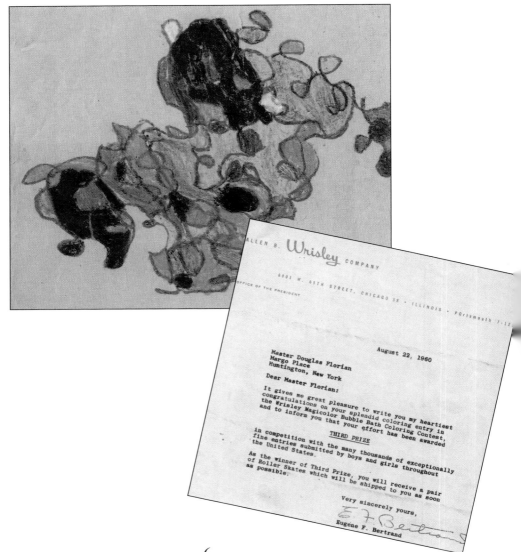

My father taught me to love nature, and to respect it
and protect it.  He taught me to see things fresh,
with my own eyes, and not to copy what other people
had already seen.

He also taught me that seeing things all around me
would help me understand the world better, and better
understand myself.

As he would say, "See for your self!"

Sometimes we would go to the Museum of Natural History, or to The Museum of Modern Art. Once at the art museum he showed me a large painting that was all black.

"What do you see, Douglas?" he asked.

"A black painting!" I replied.

He told me to look closer. Slowly, I realized there were different kinds of black: a red black and a green black. And I saw that there were geometric shapes in the painting: squares and rectangles.

I saw it for myself.

My mother also taught me many things. She taught me how to read and to love reading and writing. She's a great reader and has a huge vocabulary. She can do a very difficult crossword puzzle in a few minutes!

I think I've gotten my love of poetry and words and writing from her.

I also learned a great deal in school. My art teachers taught me to draw and paint from a model, still life, or landscape. They taught me to use shapes, colors, lines and textures to express myself.

One of my teachers would draw with so much feeling that she would sometimes tear right through the paper with her stick of charcoal! Another teacher of mine could draw with both hands at the same time.

One of my favorite teachers was Marvin Bileck, a man who was always smiling. He illustrated a beautiful Caldecott Honor book called *Rain Makes Applesauce*. It has thousands of pencil lines in it, but not one line too many.

I did hundreds of drawings while I was going to school. Here is one of an electronic man.

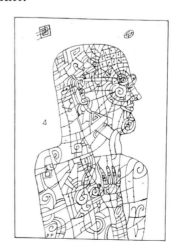

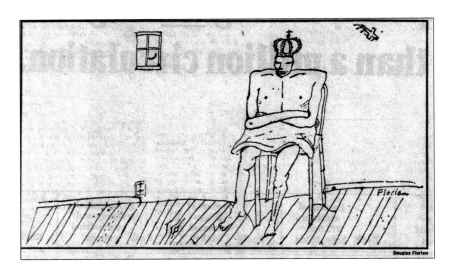

I started to do drawings for The New York Times
when I was studying art at Queens College.
This drawing illustrated an article by Prince Charles
of England.

It was a lot of fun, but working for a newspaper you have
to work very fast. Usually you only have one or two days
to do sketches and a finished piece of art.

About twenty-five years ago I started illustrating children's books. *The Night It Rained Pancakes* by Mirra Ginsberg was one of the first.

My editor asked me to write my own book, and soon I did.

*A Bird Can Fly*, showed things that animals can do and things they cannot do. For example, a bird can build a nest, but it can't build a dam. A beaver can build a dam. I think I was inspired by my love of birds and by all the birds in my neighborhood and nearby parks.

*A Bird Can Fly* did not have much success, but a later book, *A Winter Day*, did. In this book I used all my great winter memories of skating, sledding, and making a snowman. Twenty years later it is still being read and enjoyed by children.

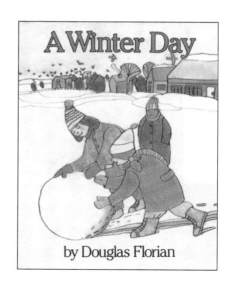

One day at a flea market I purchased a book called
*Oh, That's Ridiculous!* for one dollar. It had many funny
poems by different authors and was edited by William
Cole. I enjoyed those poems and Tomi Ungerer's
drawings so much that I decided to write my own poems
and illustrate them.

That summer I wrote about 300 poems and
created a number of drawings to go with them.
Some of those poems wound up in a book
called *Monster Motel.*

For the illustrations in the book I used pen-and-ink
and watercolor paints on a smooth paper called vellum.

I liked the way the colors would pool up on the paper
in a slightly monstrous way. Watch out for the monster
meatballs in *Monster Motel*—they bite back!

I love to write poetry. In a poem you can express your feelings, use your imagination, play with words, spell words wrong, use bad grammar, and print the poem in a funny shape.

You can do anything you want as long as it makes the poem better. That's called *poetic license*. In 1994 Harcourt Brace published one of my favorite books, *beast feast*.

We used lower case letters for the title because it seemed to be funnier and less formal. For the same reason, we put the page numbers on the side of the page instead of the bottom. The book had 21 poems and paintings about animals—some familiar, like bats and ants, and some unusual, like the rhea, a South American bird that can't fly.

When this book enjoyed a great success, my editor and I decided to do a series of poetry books on animals.

13

Another favorite of mine in the series is *insectlopedia* with paintings and poems about insects and spiders. In this book I used collage.

Artists use collage by pasting a thing on a thing on a thing. That's the *thing* of it. This book got under people's skin with its *infectious* humor. I call it my national *pestseller.*

When a book does well after some time has passed, they say it "has legs." I guess you could say *insectlopedia* "has legs," six of them, to be exact.

I work in a place called a studio. There I have tables
and chairs, paints and brushes, pens and pencils, and
different kinds of paper.

My studio has many big windows, through which I can
see the school yard of PS 111, and the children who
play there.

You may notice that my studio is a big mess, but that's the way I like it. I get more ideas for my poems and paintings by surrounding myself with pictures, rubber stamps, books, and even scraps of paper.

My studio is on the sixth floor of a very old building that used to be a piano factory. I can still hear the ghosts playing beautiful music. Actually, there aren't any ghosts there, but there are other artists. Sometimes I ask them to look at my art to see what they think.

I want my art to communicate to other people, so if something is not clear I have to do it over.

In my studio I spend time on the phone. I talk to friends
and family, and make appointments to visit artists or
schools. Then I'm ready to work.

Many of my paintings are done on paper bags, the kind you get in a grocery store.

I open a bag up at the seams, cut off the bottom, then paint it white with a paint called primer or gesso.

Gesso gets the paper ready for paint. Once the gesso is completely dry I draw lines with pencils and then paint with watercolor paints.

I use an expensive brush made from the hairs of an animal called a sable. A sable brush always has a sharp point, even when it's wet.

Sometimes I use rubber stamps in a painting,
and sometimes I paste together pieces of paper
on top of each other—collage.

I get a lot of help doing my books.
My wife and kids help me. My editor and designer
help me. And when I visit schools, the teachers,
librarians, and kids all help me.

I find out what people understand and enjoy,
what they don't understand and enjoy, and why.

Kids always ask me, "Where do you get your ideas?"
I say that I get all my ideas at Sears and Poem Depot.

Actually I get my ideas from the many different
places I go like museums, zoos, and aquariums.

I get many ideas from books I read.  I especially like field guides because they contain lots of interesting facts and photos of animals and their habitats.

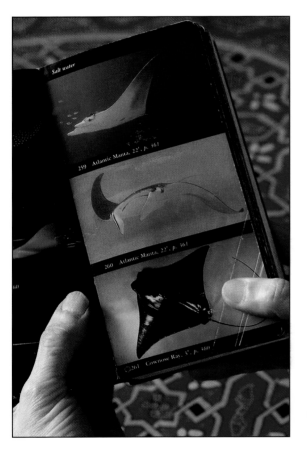

I even get ideas from a dictionary.

Did you know the word "caterpillar" is taken from
the Latin word "catta" which means cat, and "pilous"
which means hairy?  In ancient Rome they thought
a caterpillar looked like a hairy cat.  Imagine that!
I also go on the internet for facts and pictures
about nature.

After I've done my research, I'm ready to write
the poems.  Most of my poems are very short,
but even a short poem can take a long time to write.

Sometimes ideas pop right into my head, and sometimes
I let my mind wander. You have to give yourself time
and space to come up with new ideas. Each word has to
be exactly the right word and each line has to have
the right rhythm.

I first write my poems in script on lined yellow paper.

Here you can see a page where I've written several poems about sharks and bats. I might have to write five or even ten poems until I come up with a really good one.

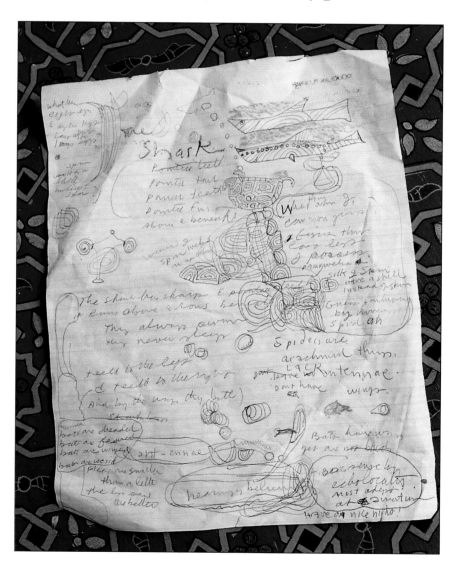

When all the poems for a book have been written,
I type them up on my computer.  Then I send them
to my editor.

My editor looks carefully at each poem and recommends
corrections.  From the fifty poems I have written,
we pick out the twenty-one best poems to include
in the book.

Then I'm ready to do the art.

In each book I like to do the art in a different way.
In *insectlopedia* the paintings look very delicate
and fragile, because insects seem that way.

In *mammalabilia* the art is simpler and bolder
because that is how mammals seem to me.

In *lizards, frogs, and polliwogs* the art got very strange and
grotesque-looking, because reptiles and amphibians look
and behave that way.

I also do abstract paintings for myself. Abstract art
doesn't illustrate any one thing specifically. Instead it
explores what color and shape and line and texture can do.

An abstract painting can mean different things to
different people. A great Swiss abstract painter named
Paul Klee once said drawing is like "taking a line for a walk."

I don't put my abstract paintings in books.
I love to show them to people in galleries
and museums, or to people who visit my studio.
You can see them at my website:
www.douglasflorian.com.

If you'd like to be an author or an artist
you might want to have an author's notebook,
or a sketchbook, or both.

Keep your eyes and ears open for sights
and sounds.

Sometimes I sketch the things I see in the neighborhood of my studio. Sometimes I go for a walk to get ideas. I might go to a bookstore, or a library, or an art museum.

I might even stop by a wall for inspiration. Here I'm touching an outdoor sculpture of an elephant.

One day I saw a painting by the artist,
Charles Cajori in an art museum. He was
my painting and drawing teacher when I was
in art school, and he taught me a great deal.

I also love to visit schools and talk to children about poetry and painting. I show them my artwork, read from my books, and discuss the different elements of poetry like rhyme, rhythm, and repetition.

I answer any questions they might have.

I always draw for the children. Sometimes I get to autograph books they have bought. I give them ideas and many times they give me ideas. I tell them to keep their eyes open, their ears open, and most importantly, their minds open.

I tell them, "See for Your Self!"
And you should too!

*Douglas Florian*

# Other Books by Douglas Florian

*Lizards, Frogs, and Pollywogs; In the Swim; Bow Wow Meow Meow: It's Raining Cats and Dogs; Bing Bang Bong; Winter Eyes; Laugh-Eteria: Poems and Drawings; On the Wing; A Beach Day; Summersaults; Autumnblings; An Auto Mechanic; City Street; Zoo's Who.*

# About the Photographer

Lee Taplinger is a freelance photographer and lives in Manhattan. His photographs have appeared in magazines, newspapers, text books, travel books, and on music CD covers in Japan where Lee lived for eighteen years.

# Acknowledgments

Photographs on pages 4, 5, 6, 7, 8, 9, 10, 11, 12, 13 (top) courtesy of Douglas Florian. Page 11 *The Night it Rained Pancakes* by Douglas Florian, copyright 1980 published by Greenwillow Books; Page 11 *A Bird Can Fly* by Douglas Florian, copyright 1980 published by Greenwillow Books; Page 11 *A Winter Day* by Douglas Florian, copyright 1987 published by Greenwillow Books, used by permission of the author. Page 12 *Monster Motel* by Douglas Florian, copyright 1993 Courtesy of Harcourt, Inc. Page 13 *beast feast* by Douglas Florian, copyright 1994 Courtesy of Harcourt, Inc. Page 14 *insectlopedia* by Douglas Florian, copyright 1998 Courtesy of Harcourt, Inc.

# Meet the Author titles

Verna Aardema  *A Bookworm Who Hatched*
David A. Adler  *My Writing Day*
Frank Asch  *One Man Show*
Joseph Bruchac  *Seeing the Circle*
Eve Bunting  *Once Upon a Time*
Lynne Cherry  *Making a Difference in the World*
Lois Ehlert  *Under My Nose*
Denise Fleming  *Maker of Things*
Douglas Florian  *See for Your Self*
Jean Fritz  *Surprising Myself*
Paul Goble  *Hau Kola Hello Friend*
Ruth Heller  *Fine Lines*
Lee Bennett Hopkins  *The Writing Bug*
James Howe  *Playing With Words*
Johanna Hurwitz  *A Dream Come True*
Eric A. Kimmel  *Tuning Up*
Karla Kuskin  *Thoughts, Pictures, and Words*
Thomas Locker  *The Man Who Paints Nature*
Jonathan London  *Tell Me a Story*
George Ella Lyon  *A Wordful Child*
Margaret Mahy  *My Mysterious World*
Rafe Martin  *A Storyteller's Story*
Patricia McKissack  *Can You Imagine*
Laura Numeroff  *If You Give an Author a Pencil*
Jerry Pallotta  *Read a Zillion Books*
Patricia Polacco  *Firetalking*
Laurence Pringle  *Nature! Wild and Wonderful*
Cynthia Rylant  *Best Wishes*
Seymour Simon  *From Paper Airplanes to Outer Space*
Mike Thaler  *Imagination*
Jean Van Leeuwen  *Growing Ideas*
Jane Yolen  *A Letter from Phoenix Farm*

For more information about the Meet the Author books
visit our website at www.RCOwen.com or call 1-800-336-5588